R SIX: The Versewagon Poetry Manual

Other poetry by the Authors

Ian McMillan: Batteries Not Included (Poetry Leeds Press 1980)
The Changing Problem (Carcanet Press 1980)
Now it can be Told (Carcanet Press 1983)
How the Hornpipe Failed (Rivelin Grapheme Press
1984)

Martyn Wiley: Just Like Eddie (Stride Publications 1983)
The Country Sundays (Littlewood Press 1985)

David Harmer: The Spinner's Final Over (Versewagon Press 1983)

John Turner: Hard Shoulders Second Home (Versewagon Press
1983)

SIX: The Versewagon Poetry Manual

Contemporary poets selected and introduced by Ian McMillan

R Rivelin Grapheme Press

ACKNOWLEDGEMENTS

The publishers wish to thank the authors and various copyright holders for permission to include some of the poems re-printed in this book including in respect of Ian McMillan CONTEMPORARY YORKSHIRE POETRY, SHEAF, CABARET 246, SOW'S EAR; in respect of David Harmer, AMBIT, STRIDE, SHEAF, BOX OF RAIN; in respect of Shirley Bell, WRITING WOMEN, NEW POETRY 8, PROOF, THE POET'S VOICE, POETRY DURHAM, GRAND PIANO ("SEA-SIDE" WON FIRST PRIZE IN OPEN UNIVERSITY POETS COMPETITION, 1983) in respect of David Horner, RAVEN, STRIDE, BBC RADIO 4, WORDS, GIANT STEPS, BOGG, GLOBAL TAPESTRY, SYDELINES.

CONTENTS

Part Five
Poems by John Turner

Part Six
Poems by David Harmer

...*an ampersand*...

INTRODUCTION

This will be short because writing an introduction to a book like this has to be the hardest part. The reading and collecting of the poems is stimulating, challenging, humbling, hilarious. But the time comes to answer questions: why these poets? why these poems?

The core of the book is Versewagon, the world's only mobile writing workshop, started in 1982 by Martyn Wiley, John Turner and myself. David Harmer has worked with Versewagon as a tutor; I met Shirley Bell at a Versewagon day in Boston, and I met David Horner while I was Writer-in-Residence at Padgate in Cheshire.

So in a sense this is a very personal anthology. I have to say, though, that I'm not attempting to usher in a new era. I'm not insisting that we are going to be the big poets of the next twenty years, the one's who'll be prominently featured in the Penguin Laser Disc of Contemporary Verse in 2008.

What we have got here are voices that will continue to be heard as the eighties grind on into the nineties. Perhaps beyond. If I can use a shop-soiled phrase, all human life is here. I wish that all poetry could grip personal and wider issues as hard as they are gripped in this book.

That's all. I hope you enjoy the book.

Ian McMillan
South Yorkshire, February 1985.

two tractors knit a field ..

PART ONE

Poems by David Horner

...three crows squatted...

DELIVERED

The farmer's got a new Ford Sierra
GL. He strokes the red-as-lipstick curves,
Fondles the upholstery's dark, tufted pile;
    A squeeze of one switch

And the aerial is roused, stands up, pricks
The air, and warm music spills out over
All the musky inside. While out beyond
    The back of his yard

The poor cow is up on her feet again
After the birth: a great big black and white
Job, like a primitive console tv,
    Fixed to trim, splayed legs.

The tail hangs thick as cable, ends in a
Tangle of coppery wires; the udder
Glows; her teats are waiting, proud, impatient
    For the turning-on.

THE BLIND MAN IN SCHOOL

Paul, with new crutches, is cock of the walk;
Letting two act panto pirates; or one
A fairground stiltman; then in laughing turns
Each play the fastest cripple in the world.
Exclusive as the fingers in your fist
Are the girls in their gathering. Elaine,
She sees, is queen in her bright new bangle:
Tomorrow there'll be one on every wrist.

And today will bring the blind man to school.
He'll come to talk, as he's done for many
Years now, to the children. He will explain
That he's just like us, but blind. He will
Ask can we see alright all he has brought here;
He'll smile and show off the wares and the tools
Of his blindman's trade. Like a fallen fledgling
They'll hold him there; together they'll whisper

Yes; gaze on him, be near to tears, wish they
Could have books with pimples, wear sunglasses
All day; know it rains by some smart machine's
Tick; own that fantastic, foldaway stick!
Tomorrow, when the sharp December hail
Strikes our windows, in its million fragments
Of shattered white sticks, we'll wake as one in
The darkness, fumble for the day in braille.

PIGS

Are glamorous: their nudity so thrills
Us, so assails, we cannot turn our eyes away.
They make of food and family life
A permanent party; thrust down upon
The trough their backs are so many
Upturned thighs, their backsides hot knees;
And such strong and dainty legs and ankles
Jammed forever in those teetering high heels.

A man can comprehend tarts and rape;
Will be almost loving with the breast
Of his cow, proffered discreetly
From under the coat. In sideburns
Permanent as dry-stone walls, the shepherd
Can get a firm hold on his ewe
From behind; can force her coat from her,
Roam and know every inch of her flesh.

But a pig is all too brazenly bare,
Snout in the air; gets what's coming to her,
Like a wife a man can't lie easy with:
She's gawped at, fed, indulged, then taken
By night; for revenge slit in two, cut
To hidable, unrecognizable bits.
In condoms we bury her poor, spent atoms.
Cured, we stuff her down our throats.

THREE POEMS NOBODY WANTED TO WRITE

1.

No-one writes a poem about
An abandoned car:
Left to settle, comfy as a hippo in mud.
Peeling stickers hint at younger days:
Scarborough, Derbyshire, Poole, Penzance.

Decay lives there now, fat cats, kids' games,
While ignorant spiders spin veils of death
Over its gaping frame.

Water, petrol, air, oil – all gone –
All gone that former life's blood.
While the rust moves over its flesh and bones,
A restless army of ants.

2.

Nobody writes a poem about
A wooden clothes peg:
A wee wooden man, a gipsy's gift;
A wild madcap ballet he can,
Can dance on your line.

But left out in all weathers,
They must huddle together –
Dull, sodden lads beside their
Oh-so-shiney-mixed-and-multi-coloured-super-spring-loaded-
Sold-at-the-supermarket-plastic-brothers.

Do they feel as they hang there
They're losing their grip?

3.

No-one writes a poem about our cherry tree
In Winter. Here, in our street, this cherry tree
In Winter. Someone should, it's quite a tree!

In May you can't miss it: a hand upturned. (Don't blink
Now!) First there's some wholly imperceptible flick
Of the wrist and – whole bouquets of pink
Flowers. Okay, I know, you see it all the time, at home, on tv –
But here, on stage, in person, live, it really is still some trick;
His once and only trick, performed each May, for us, free.

But in Winter he plays the Tragedy King, pathetic.
We are but indifferent daughters. The hand
Suppliant, a cup of cold, arthritic.
Yet in truth we've a wizard lying under our street,
A Giant's frame at rest beneath our land.
Our houses are his sepulchre, our earth his winding sheet.

So no-one writes a poem about our cherry tree
In Winter. If one of us would, we all perhaps could;
Then walk beneath, around his every single splinter
And knuckle, and read our poems there, out loud
For him who is quiet, our tree, this Winter.

POSTCARDS FROM THE PIER'S END

1.

She's seated, sleeping.
Her husband's painting the sea.
Pictures on canvas.

2.

On the pier's end rail
In tan boots leans a cowboy
All those white horses!

3.

This wife is shining,
Reading her Georgette Heyer.
A closed book to him.

4.

This earth's a ballroom!
Here on the floor's margin the
Partnerless walk free.

5.

False teeth chew soft bread
Each noon on the wooden pier.
Hark! Death Watch Beetle!

6.

The red phone booth sweats.
Cold white fingers poke through pain.
And at the third stroke.

7.

The sea comes up, waves.
The old couple stare and stare
Not sure it's for them.

SECOND CHILDHOOD

Take the very last episode of all:
Jerry on his own at the wheel, small
In his slinky, pink limo, as we go
Past the same tree, the same tree, the same tree, oh
And the skies are darkening all the time,

To a mountain, signposted Bare Skull Hill.
Electric doors open, we enter and, well
It's all just the usual Top Secret scene:
Pastel walls, men in tunics, blue, khaki, green.
I could be bored in a place like that.

Neat in his three-button business suit,
As military high-ups, respectful, salute,
The mouse steps out and curls one small finger,
White-gloved, diamond-ringed, round a neat trigger.
We watch a pointer shiver to the zero.

You have to imagine you're at Tom's place now:
The customary, one from any, wood frame house.
The rocket in flight – you know it's for Tom –
Past the same cloud, the same cloud, the same cloud, comes
Then there's all the routine sound-effects, till

Tom appears, fur peeling like cigarette
Paper, head glowing red; he just flies straight
Up and out through the hole the rocket made in the first
Place, lips tight gripped, eyes swelling, going to burst.
Then all the howling and shrieking that you always get.

He's a mass of tiny flames as he descends.
The town's out, looking up at the sight, hands
Raised to shield their eyes from the light, and
Briefly the fiery fragments linger, to land
Like feathers, making of each man's fingers candles.
I'm afraid we just sat watching helpless.

THE HAVEN OF ANIMALS
for James Dickey

When the young bulls first rose up
To nose out her garden she was already
Stinking all the way out to her
Death. Impatient at the winter's
Mealy-mild months, the flesh

Had gone before. Her skin drily
Glinting was tautening daily, vacuum
Packing her bone by soft
Bone. Joints were seizing
In parting handshakes without end.

When the young bulls first entered
Her garden – coming silent and careful,
Their breath in big bouquets before
Them, they like reborn meteoric stones –
She was sleeping, leaving

Only the frog-eyes of bulging
Bone-knuckles to keep watch over her.
Her lungs were winter
Trees; her breathing like
Empty wagons bound for Warsaw

Over frozen points. And she slept
As they sauntered there, slept then woke
To a sky sheer white
And she rising at last
Through snow. On knurled

Fists wrought to the forms
Of roots of ginger; on arms as frail
As dog shit sticks, she hauled:
To gaze where the snow
Now gestured her, out

To where, trampling the
Order of her garden the young bulls
Ranged, each sinking his legs
In the slush-mulched earth
A full pizzle's length

Or more. Nuzzling for bulb
Globes; rending the Lamb's Ear; grass
And lost apple made delicious
Flesh. Their mudded flanks
Fair, firm and easy

On earth and air. Trembling
To the slap and suck and slide of them,
Allowing their crunch and
Crush to fall on her,
Rinse and rise in her like

Spring rain and tide, till
Falling to sleep, thoroughly filled
And flushed withal. Later, dull
Boots would trudge to reclaim
Them; caring voices would climb

And find her shockingly
Abandoned, so they believed. On sheets
As grey as rotting snow
Her bare bones had formed
To a single, perfect arch.

THE VIEWING

These were never naughty in school;
Where they have been sent they have stayed.
Their rooms in this home are boxed neat
As closed books, each one a can of
        Shadows.

Their air is dyed to mafia black;
They keep their own and loved ones close.
A man sits side on at his window;
She faces front: neighbours making
        Mugshots.

A woman is waving to me;
She is small in the frame's corner.
The moving of her arm is less
Than the shifting of dust through cold
        Sunlight.

Her mouth's a mail box. Another
Waves, and there one more: a flourish
Fine as Brueghel has Icarus'
Legs, busking unnoticed through green
        Water.

All this is not graffiti. Here
Are not the clichés of writing
On the wall. It is the adding
Of signature to a finished
        Portrait.

That man sits still. Back hunched full as
A boxer's glove. Huge as Wordsworth's cliff
That night in Patterdale. He looks
And I steal shied away in my
        Small boat.

SEMINARY

Like gobs full of rocks are the farm-shop
Freezers: inarticulate through the shards
They smoke and grate their intention to strop
Men's fingers if stroked too long or too hard.
Runs to the circling sky the melt-water
In spokes. The sun will lie low in the copse
All day: a coin on each pane of the house.
And her eyes are like spiders in winter

As, come for the first time, she sees May stride
And part penned turkeys like mere bracken, soon
Drawing some cock-bird down upon a wide
Lap; to cluck, and chuck his gulping throat; croon
And caress all fears away. The small skull
Of pumice; the scorched throat where, scrotal, hang
Warts above bristling hair. And all the young
Shyness of that proud, stiffened neck, until

The head flies away like a bottle cap.
Vomit giggles in her mouth and hot blood
Pouts on her white apron. Done, and May slaps
The great sow in passing to the plucking shed
And its sound rings round like applause. May's hands,
She recalls, are green, as she holds the steel
Cutters May'd so casually let fall, feels
Metal adorn her, becoming a woman.

STONE
for Alan Howe

Where the tide could not quite touch
The sandstone pebbles had glowed, ripe
As plums, honey-filled glass ampoules.
Fixed on cliff mud those ammonites
Had seemed so many endless smiles.

High in this deserted quarry,
Scooped to the limit of the land's
First ridge, the stone is growing soft:
Chalk melts to wet dough; the slate's long
Been drawn and the folds of shale stand
No firmer than an old man's gum.

The grasses flex like bandsaw blades;
Everywhere the heathers cower;
Like rags sparse petals hang from gorse –
It rears in fixed and silent mobs,
Petrified on the quarry floor.

Below, two tractors knit a field;
The fine dust thus combed out first lifts,
Runs back across the finished earth,
Over sheep set out like boulders –
To settle where the tide has now
Roofed to the shore line, slate on slate.

LADY FRANKENSTEIN

's the only one everyone in our town knows:
Knows the mad and faddish way she buffets at
The bins: emptied tins, banana skins, those
Sandwiches she pries into like other folk's love
Letters; hungers after knowing where she's stuffed
Her fortune; knows she is familiar with cats.

It's said that men and bears both walk the same.
She pads the streets. The flies follow after her,
Licking her lips. The children yell out her name
And flirt. Adults look on, as bored as cushions;
Or else our thin and sideways eyeing is the pins,
It seems, that hold her bones and rags together.

For we give her her existence. She is as a hair
In the mouth. We breathe life into her. She's fed
Our thoughts; has assumed our voice. Her stare
Phosphorates the soul. Her breath is Asia. The space
Round her is our horizon. Mapped her face
With earthy tracks down which all the wretched tread.

We turn, as once when mineshafts first in England
Plumbed their grounds, rich men withdrew, afraid, discreet;
When the first black pithead, bearlike, reared on their land,
To their rearmost rooms they withdrew, looked away;
And fires burned – for the while kept cold and dark at bay.
And the earthworks closing in, coming to their feet.

When she dies we will send our children to enter
Her house. They'll rip out wire like veins; peel plaster
Like failed flesh; the pipes will throw up plasma.
She is always the one we none of us invite:
The one who is with us on all our wedding nights.
She will pad the streets. She is not the monster.

for Liz Lochhead

ADVERT FOR ADVENT

Narcissus' false finger nails come clawing the dark;
He's drowning in earth that is chocolate black.

Visible as icebergs, men stream to work.
Cars turn over, will not be roused, or hack
Cruelly on the first smoke of the day.
At this hour all the houses have bad breath.

Water breaks cover – makes a getaway;
Snowflakes crowd, hurl themselves to certain death.

Later, those left behind for all to see –
(Grey ghosts on grey corners – the old, the young) –
Will gather, grins grimaced into place, scree-
Flakes to the mountain's bleak base fallen, flung.

But now the good wife's backside – gentle, early –
Comes, a beachball to his sleeping belly.

PLAINSONG FOR CHRISTMAS EVE

The hour is late; the men
Are in the gents, inventing themselves.
Piss steams like a donkey's breath, staggers
Off like a drunk in a snowfield from pricks
     As limp as windsocks,
Pointing to nowhere in particular.

On neat legs the women
Wait – impregnable as holly trees.
Outside under a threadbare sky lads
Stamp and bawl choruses; bounce their voices
     Off parked cars, mute walls,
Heaven; rejoice to hear themselves returned.

We are all wrapped up, know
What to expect. A tyre tossed up a
Lamppost glows for a halo. The moon's
Like a rejected coin in a call-box.
         A jetplane pulses
Flat and even across the night's blank screen.

Our walking home is as
The small stirrings of life in some great
Symphony's pauses. Behind the pub
A snowman stands, an ampersand at the
         Conjunction of sky
And land, for this and every silent night.

MUSEUM-PEACE

*". . . the faces of Strangers are but moving Portraits – and far from my
comfortable little cottage I feel as if I were in the long damp Gallery of some
Nobleman's House."*
                    Coleridge, in a letter to Josiah Wade, 1796

The doors are always by Escher:
They turn and return forever;

There's only going round again;
They pull, or is it push, you in.

(Past this entrance the children can't
Make head – nor tail – of busts that aren't.)

Madonnas, dead nobs, nipples stare
Their urbane patronage; and there

At each stair-turn the guardians wait;
Uniforms hide them like the night;

Their buttons eye-spy us as we pass.
Humility is tyrannous

In these who offer from their sheaf
Of handouts, just one, like a leaf

26

To cover us in poor exchange
For goods and clothes. We stand estranged,

Left to shiver in flesh that must
Feign buckram. They have a genius

For keeping us together here
In one's and two's. We whisper,

And our sentences are endless,
Crude beside their dumb finesse.

One stands by sheer, glass, frameless doors,
And out there, after many more

Such, stands another, assistant
To perfected art: so distant

Or can it be he is as near
As is reflexion? Facial hair

Is carved on each like topiary.
We shuffle in society

Most secret. We climb, feel buried
Beneath, it seems, The Pyramids;

Their crossing our paths binds us close
As mummies. We feel ourselves gross

And as unnatural as trees.
They've cut us lovingly to size

And shape; they've handled us with pride;
And all the while we know, outside,

The cold air will walk to us, take
Our faces, smack us wide awake.

In frameless glasses comes the torturer.
A uniform's a sheath, a silencer.

THE AUTUMN BESTIARY

River creeps; is near to sleep; flat of foot.
Her snail-trails are left in ditches for dead.
This season's alchemy turns all to lead.

The very last apple's perched in a tree;
Hard as a snowball, green ice to its core.
While those we've rescued lie melting in drawers.

With stick a child provokes a weary fire –
Rose heads, clods of earth, glacéd leaves, soft logs –
Till smoke crawls off like some distempered dog.

Silence floods the brain at a mower's stop.
Dragged backwards, the sounds loosed from its mouth
Are the faint cries of birds lost to the south.

As refugees the trees walk. Leaves hang like
Hands and mean wrists of men dead on barbed wire,
Or are footprints in mud, poulticed with fire.

With gimlet-thin legs cows screw down the earth.
Sheep shit shot. Cows perform a meringue base,
And dance *l'homage à Pavlova* with grace.

A sneeze becomes a custard pie. This last
Blue sky will kill your mother for the joke:
"The smyler with the knyf under the cloke."

COMING TO TERMS

"Writing is also speech without an interlocutor, addressed to an absent or imaginary person or to no-one in particular – a situation new and strange to the child."

(L. S. Vygotsky 'Thought and Language')

We can't all keep our Dinky Toys; get born
A Jew; invent and then denounce The Bomb;
Have grandads each a hero of the Somme;
Construe the cosmos from a West Coast lawn;
Nor live in Paris flats in exile, from
Which we face the East; resist as outworn
The imagery of Ruth's *sad heart*, yet mourn
The kissing, hot beneath the tanks of home.
The man next door has long since been dismissed.
He saves the cards you get with tea: remote
Kings; Tensing and the flag on Everest;
He offers London burning, Captain Oates,
The Globe to his kids. "History," he insists;
His voice, like each turned card, a small footnote.

GIRL IN RED TROUSERS

This far into summer, and the sun's near
Spent; has given his all to land he'll soon
Abandon, as the lover the older
Woman's slackening belly. Like a birth scar
Runs the railway on this bridge in the noon
Heat; steel, timber and cement: regular
In their solid geometry. Young boys mass
Here, sit on high and wait for what must pass.

Beneath the rails, between the walls is ripe
With an absence, boxed up like a great djin
In some tale; and like a huge beast asleep
A pool is spread on the floor, at home,
Familiar; in there stands a girl in
Red trousers – forced to one side to become
Her own shadow by a cyclist's blind shove
Into the dark and the train's slow grind above.

Both done, she enters the water to wait
Till at last on its silent, slow-clearing screen
She there can watch herself take shape, grow straight
Downward, see she says she all the way through
Like rock. Her skipping out makes tambourine
Smacks that pick up the train's dying tattoo.
The boys sit, heads turned, still; their backsides gaze
Down, and all man's world's progressing sideways.

THE ASCENT OF MAN

Our man has a wife and one small daughter,
Lives in a small town in provincial Japan;
By day and to keep all their bodies together
He's a teacher of music: classical guitar.

But then once night is properly fallen
And the singing of the street lamps is done –
Up and out and onto the roof of his flat-topped house,
Softly,
In self-made, battery-heated slippers,
Softly,
He climbs and alone there on the floor of the roof
Of his flat-topped house he sits,
And with binoculars and trusted home-made telescope
He hunts.

Comets are his particular prey –
Comets as they arch and dive.
So far he's cornered, caught, (and each one
Brand flaming new, live
And wooshy-tailed) 5!

Then reined together full forty eight hours
His comet and he, onward as one,
They ride through the wild and cactus-sharp stars
In a life-long rush to the Sun.

THE OLD WIFE'S TALE

Old Mrs. Beatty she wasn't all there:
She took *The Tatler*, every evening walked alone;
Like a summer's dawn's mist thinning, her hair.
In the clouds our elders' voices droned:
Discreet their chorus to our shrill, clear line.
Old Mrs. Beatty she's a child in a bonfire – black ash etching the air.

Old Mrs. Beatty had a screw loose:
She could make the chewing gum slip and wrap
Tight round your ribs, tight as the laces in grandad's boots;
She could make the great steel fridge in Sharp the grocer's shop stop,
Stop your heart beneath Sharp's cunning grin.
Old Mrs. Beatty she's a jar of dead minnows – your hand on the noose.

Old Mrs. Beatty was mad:
There, in autumn, in her pale square of garden her one
Tree would flare up berries – good,
Red, hard as knuckle for the fighting. To lick one
Was death. To bite one was death. The golden hairs
On their inside could ease and wriggle through skin to your blood.
Old Mrs. Beatty she's a gang full of whispers – each balaclava a hanged
man's hood.

Old Mrs. Beatty was possessed:
One morning, one spring, she took me: dry
Fingers on bare arm. (Her touch sowed warts). Voices, she pressed,
Were calling to her. Was it I?
Calling on the cold, cruel lips of her letterbox. Was it I? Was it I?
Old Mrs. Beatty, she's a dead witch now, buried now at last.
Old Mrs. Beatty, she's a spider held in amber – twitching, tickling,
cannot rest.

THEY ALSO SERVE

In a flagrance of shades and adulterous buttons
They're out. School is over and one run-shouts
To her lady-in-waiting. "Did no work today! Didn't do
Nothing! We just painted, watched newts, sang the walls away!"

Pressed against the railings like the sad child
I'the story, he waits odd days, this
Dad. The talk does hold that he has no *proper* job. "Does
Nothing. He's an artist. I can't imagine what he does all day."

So many mammals, sea-wearied, up for air, the mums
Are met; beached in these their winter coats
Their common chorus spuming up in clumps. "Did
Nothing. Spring-cleaned the postman, talked with the house,"
they say.

JUNTA

Perspective lends enchantment to the view
As on the military government's official photograph
The president erect in his colonel-in-chief's uniform
And behind him the armed forces' triumvirate
In theirs, resemble nothing so much as
The handle and prongs of a toasting fork.

And above this, the tips of those glittering caps
Just piercing, hangs a wooden framed
Madonna and Child, attentive and dark.

The poor cow...

PART TWO

Poems by Martyn Wiley

... " careful stares " ...

THE NEW YORKSHIRE LANDSCAPES

1. YEAR

This is the year, the year of the line,
a moving line.

This is the year, the year of the vans
moving in lines.

This is the year, the year of the shield
the year of the stick beating the shield.

This is the year, the year of the shout
the year of the bottle caught in the light.

This is the year, the year of the horse
the year of the hooves clattering the streets.

This is the year, the year of the dog
on back legs and chain
waiting to bite.

(CORTONWOOD NOV 1984)

2. ROADBLOCK

A fin de siecle morning
with a pheasant killing mist.

The shooting parties are long gone
in a rattle of hobnail and brogue;
the big house stands shuttered
holding only the old men from the war
who will spend all their mornings
walking.

At the main road we wait
where we always wait
but this morning a motorbike cop
stands with his arm raised
against the buzzing traffic.

A pause; breath hanging,
before eight blue vans
dark as gangsters in shades
sweep into and out of focus
away down the lane.

The cop lowers a gauntletted fist
covers his half hidden face
and is gone.

(HICKLETON, SOUTH YORKSHIRE)

3. MORNING

I could write about the morning
brisk and blue.

I could write about these trees
brittle in white embroidery.

I could write about the turn of a year
the passing of time

Or I could write about silent winding gear
and men warming their hands on a fire

Under the careful stares of policemen
all stamping their feet like men at a match.

(PRINCE OF WALES COLLIERY, NEW YEARS EVE 1984)

4. TRAIN SPOTTING

Every morning they are here
watching
Ten of them in a hired van
waiting
at the top of our lane
where we went to watch trains
watching
summer days hang loose like washing
waiting
for the dinner time 'Devonian'
and tea time 'Thames-Clyde'
watching
reinforcements slide into position
dogs in the back
watching
pitmen in donkey jackets
with ironic NCB's on the back
waiting.

(DEARNE VALLEY, SUMMER 1984)

5. COALPICKERPICKEDABADBAG

This morning I saw a man
kneeling in the road

By his side a bicycle
one wheel still spinning

On the ground a plastic sack
split like sausage skin.

The man was scooping sleck
between his hands

Gathering muck into his lap
the face streaked black.

On any other day, in any other town
it might have been funny.

(CASTLEFORD 1985)

NIGHT SHIFT

That sky was the colour of a smacked eye
as a guzzling pub spilled into the street
its one braying voice in praise of the heat
and inside the mesters in caps and ties
stare into clouds of hanging blue smoke
all ignoring their white cardied wives with
laquered hard hats of Friday night hair
and young men in shirts all cracking their jokes
all cracking their jokes and having a crack
days afters nights the bastard nights
of beer on to a club into a fight
with Walt who says their lass won't have him back.

We heard them coming a long way away
over the top of Elvis Presley's voice
(In The Ghetto) before giving no choice
but to shut it and gawp as they hee hawed past
with red white and blue light flashing on glass.

Five dead. Thirty injured. Gas.

FORTY WEEKS

The house falls silent
everything is ready.

Your room sleeps in the sun
red geraniums reaching out.

Anytime now and despite the summer
we will light you a fire.

You have travelled forty weeks
through the darkness.

Soon you will begin
and everything is ready
even the silence.

WAITING

Three hours before he was born
they moved us into a room with a view

of a bed and a chair and a long window
of a discarded thriller by Ed McBain
still open, spine broken, at page fourteen.

Outside, a softly poached sun
begins to warm the sleepy town
as you clutch air through a mask
and quiet nurses come and go

To a bed and a chair and a long window
to a discarded thriller by Ed McBain
still open, spine broken, at page sixteen.

MORNING HAS BROKEN

6

These buildings huddle together for warmth
around concrete spaces where flowers were
never seriously considered and
where cold cars sit frosted with their eyes glazed
blank under white hats that somehow seem right.

Across the way the first trains are rattling
through an empty station where the name boards
got carried away making this whole place
nowhere again for the faces the faces
that stare into papers hoping for news.

Inside, the shiny kitchens are steaming
and sweating down stainless steel as the first
trolleys are pushed away down corridors
where glass polished floors reflect all the light
always the light from outside and in as
the lifts come to life.

7

Upstairs Geoff is sitting cross legged on the
carpet outstaring the fish as they swim
round the tank oblivious of him
rocking and singing continuous songs
from the shows that he never saw until
he catches a glimpse in the glass of a nurse
asking him something from far away

Faraway, Lucy's faraway from this
listening to the voices as they start
again quieter than before but still
there still talking insisting that she's wrong
about them, always wrong, always wrong Tom
is talking to the nurses and smiling
he's telling them it's alright he wants to
go home with the plasters fresh on his throat.
A fat girl is laughing into her tea
it is a funny cup of tea and she
can't stop laughing or crying, this morning
in the office they are rattling their keys
end of the shift, another one done, go

8

Down below cars are filling the spaces
between white lines as the snow comes harder.
Another morning has crawled in unseen
watching red buses and slow traffic pass
in a flick book flicker beyond the rails
of green painted fences that stretch for miles
marking the boundaries without a smile.

Men in caps are clearing the paths, keeping
a track for the white coats to cross and for
the shuffling men in overgrown macs who
try to roll fags with blue ataxic hands.
Asphasic and echolalic they walk
alone in pairs down the dark paths of home
twenty, thirty, fifty years alone
in a crowd and alone in a coat that
was bought for no one and is worn by all.

Breakfast is served in the house on the hill
where the knives rattle loud on crested plates
and beyond the green gates is outer space.

LATE NEWS ITEM

At the border we stopped;
you wiped lipstick from the windscreen.

At the hotel we cupped our secret
like a flame between hands.

At the cottage it was simple
bright sun on white walls.

Driving home, at night, we hear
that Elvis is dead.

The headlights cut slices from the dark
but it stays dark.

IN AMERICA

I was there once;
and every morning
I was still dreaming.

Flicking across fifteen channels
at six am
scooping ice from a bin
and slicing Manhattan with the blinds.
Walking down Broadway
eating pastrami on rye
as the yellow cabs came up with the sun
and the steam started to rise.

Another time, out on the cape
we ate fried chicken
under the boardwalk
and drank cold Budweiser
with a man who told us
that here the greenback talked
and if you got greenbacks
then you are somebody.

There was breakfast
at a truck stop in Maine
where the sun was already high
over guys in baseball caps
where they called your name
down a crackling p.a.
when the order was ready to go
and you felt like somebody.

THE LAST BUFFALO

This is not the wild west;
there is no piano swinging
in time to the doors
as boot meets face.
The frontiersmen are back
seeking buffalo
as boot meets face.

This is not Graham Greene;
you are not the European
with a four day beard
sweating in his room
and trying not to hear the screams
as stick meets back.
Clouds of dust swirl into town
scattering the sidewalks.
Take a root beer and kill the taste
or smear blueberry pie
into the cuts on your face.

This is not the late late show;
there is no TV dinner
the ice box has broken down
spilling buffalo meat into the street
as bullet meets brain.
Jeeps bump by with guns held high
like candles on a cake
They have chased the last buffalo
into a saloon and now we wait
so crack another Coke
feel the can cool on your brow
as bullet meets brain.

STAND BY YOUR MAN

It spilled into the road like a runaway scrum
with its jackets all jingling and flannels a flap
as its small change went flying on shiny tarmac
and a brylcreem bouncing bonce pulled down the full moon.

'Ey, eyup, watch it, who tha lookin at bastard,
tha lookin at me, ah thee, tha'd better not be
cos if thi are tha'll get a crack straight across it'

At the end of the road all the cars rev away
passing the fat lass and her mate in day glo socks
who play the bandit in a blue neon chip shop
as a black and white dog pisses against a post
and a bloke in his fifties knocks dust from his coat.

11 PLUS

We spent all afternoon buying the uniform
buying an entire list from blazer to vests
all crackle-wrapped in paper and string
under the whizzing of overhead tracks
and the chanting of my mother's Co op number.

On our way home
she insisted that I learn to use a phone.
I still remember the weight of that door
as it sealed us in
the thin skitter of pages
the trick with coins and a dial
and my father's voice distant
breathing a cheap perfume
all of us knowing but none of us saying
that the boy was going away.

A SUITABLE CASE

On slow afternoons
he would wrestle his brushes
back into their bulging case
packing them tight
between sparkle clean creams
and the violet gleam
of WINDOLENE.

Then, relaxing,
he would talk of his friend
Jesus.
He had not met Jesus but rather
taken him into his life
somewhere in the Yorkshire Dales
so that now they walked together
and he himself was filled with joy;
a crackling cellophane wrapped thing
straining the rusty locks of his case.

Sometimes he left a tract
or a new toothbrush;
always I searched the street
for Jesus.

FOUR HOUSES AREN'T ALWAYS AN HOTEL

The sky has lost its credibility
hanging, Kodachrome blue, between lintels
like an empty swimming pool.

Awkward on crimson Chesterfields
we are listening to the sky
and George who works for ICI
and oh the rates in Manchester
are so incredibly high
I mean a thousand a year
for a quite ordinary semi.

Outside, the trees are draining away
dressing the lawn in cock pheasant shades
and Sally is still at the Poly
though Newcastle's not quite as jolly
as she thought it was going to be.

The window is turning outside in
to a Landseer print of guests at bay
as night gathers momentum behind
the epic story of their son
John at UCLA.

AT THE CLOUDS WITH HENRI

The whitest wall
slabbed against blue sky.

The grinning dog
holding him on a string

And him sliding down the car
like snow from a roof.

The dog pulls the string
and his mouth moves.

I am prepared
I will not understand
it will be easier.

*'Je ne complet, monsieur
je suis anglais'*

Clouds collide
around the dog's eyes.

I am not full mister
I am English.

PICTURE FRAMING

Under our feet, the river oozes past
silent as measured medicine.

Above our heads, the circling gulls
easy on white vests
like men on doorsteps.

On a hotel balcony,
between river and gulls
six chefs are standing

Watching us watching
they all start waving
as we frame the print
and walk away.

THE VIDEO OF OUR SHOW

The poet wears a green shirt;
counts the five trees
outside his window
and watches children walking by.

The poet wears a red shirt;
he is watching the trains
watching blue screens flashing up names
as station announcers
fumble their lines.

The poet wears a blue shirt;
lights a fake cigarette
with a joke lighter
as the motorway splashes
black coffee on white tables.

The poet wears a yellow shirt;
climbs the hundred steps
into an empty theatre
where a red plush silence
is caught in the lights.

THE NIGHT OF THE LONG NIGHTS

'ALL TRANSISTOR' etched in red
between dashboard and road
where cats eyes wait to meet
the coughed out gale warnings
that sweep across the fens.
It's now that the heater loses heat.
Pass me that stick, wrong end first.

This is a fancy dress warning
set your watch by the horns on that Viking
Ten to two. Another breakfast before bed.

A left hook from a phone box door
knocks you into an asteroid machine
where you can't even begin
to count the stars of a world service night
sharing its football scores
with an African dawn
down there in corridors
tiled with ice.

Pass me that stick.

DIFFERENT DREAMS

Suddenly it arrived
dropping down the neat rows
of flowering chimneys
with its galloping horses
wide open prairies
and vertical cities.

It shone a flickering light
onto pale November faces
then flung us three thousand miles
to the west and left us
to make our own way home.

AT THE POINT OF HAPPINESS

This is not just another poem
about Vincent Van Gogh.
I don't want to talk about a sky
of crows over cornfields,
white bridges or blue flowers
because this morning
in the Van Gogh Museum
all the pictures have been released
sprung from their heavy frames
into the frosty streets
where they flash in the windows of trams
and melt the ice in the canals
their warm oil oozing and flowing
down tall gabled walls
surprising the staid green doors
with splashes of gold
as we stand, holding hands
at the point of happiness.

EATING OUT

I was convinced that this was the place
I told her I'd read about it
in the Good Food Guide,
told her it was unpretentiously English
with a discreet ambience.

Outside, I pointed to the hand written menu
a feature of this place's intrinsic charm
and confessed I couldn't recall the chef's name
but was sure that he had trained under Anton Mosiman
it had been in The Guardian.

Inside, I notice that there are no chairs
at the bar three men with long hair
are shouting the word 'fuck'
Behind the bar a fat man in a Tshirt
is watching Tom and Jerry cartoons
on a black and white with the sound down.
Eyes elsewhere he floods a glass with beer
then cuts a finger, BASTARD, slicing lemon
for her drink.

Later, I have curry and she has a pizza
(the curry contains bright green peas)
the pizza shatters over the bar
where nobody notices.
I study the barman's tattoos.

THAT WORKSHOP ELEMENT

Putting aside my poems . . .

'The courses are excellent,
first rate, tip top'
Last year she did writing for pleasure
and the thriller.

She has not, herself, written anything
for many years but recently bought
an electric type writer.

She will send me all the details
and I really ought to try and apply
because as a beginner and a man
I may well be offered a place.

Picking up my poems . . .

„ringing ringing"

PART THREE

Poems by Ian McMillan

— The small leader...

RESIDENT

"There's a bloke there reading a book"
"I don't give a shit"

The view from the study window
never changes.

There is always the pit, always the scaffolding yard,
always a wagon loaded with battens.

Usually the rain. Usually
my family, her family,
spreading back across the yard,
usually Harry, dead six months,
Pete, walking his dog, Garry and Val,
and Darryl, and Harry, usually,
dead six months, and Pete,

and they say "Do you have time to write?"

I am writing this, on a train going through Irlam.

Every house on a certain street
for sale.
A white pony in a field of gorse.

On Piccadilly Station,
walking with her son,
between platform four and platform five

Is a woman with a well-trimmed beard.

Do you have time to write?
I am writing this.

"He's writing in the book now."
"I still don't give a shit."

THE MONSTER'S LAST LETTERS TO HIS CHILDREN

"The bolty and the stitchy bloke
is sitting at his desk . . ."

A duck, my lads,
laid
in waddling clothes
miles from the sea
months from the water.

Avast there! Wandering
the sunset plank
like a drunk.

The sun has got his balaclava on
back to front.

My dear sons.
Christmas like this
brings on the big sobs.

Boys, I'm sorry.
I should be a better father,
make you laugh.

Watch this card trick: you
take a card, any card. You
memorise it and then.

I forget. I have the deck
in front of me and I forget!

I'm sorry. Night pulls
the teeth of day;
I'm not a monster, boys.
I'm a poetry.

He's got me covered. Listen:
"Love poem. Her eyes
were like three crows in a cornfield
and when she spoke it was like
three crows in a cornfield.
She undressed, and three crows
squatted in a cornfield."

He's bound me hand and foot,
the Doctor Frankenstein,
stitched me to myself.

Lads I'm not a monster
I'm a secondhand tent.

Night pulls the teeth of day
scatters them over the sky
like three crows in a cornfield.

I finished the love story
lines ago in the white.

Lads I am your affectionate father
who is not a monster but a poetry.

You are too young to understand,
my children.

I'm a nut, fellers.
I'm Phil O'Sparks
the Tortured Torso;
I'm slipping away.

I've been beaten on the soles of my feet
repeatedly for three months
with a heavy concrete floor
and I am still nowhere,

miles away across the black
woods and the white walls.

"I ate twelve moths
in a year, sizzling
in the mouth's flame"

(Not a monster but a poetry!)

I have been deprived of sleep
for sixty-five days
and my dreams are queueing up
behind the cell door.
A guard is busking
up and down the line
with tap shoes and a violin

and my dreams
are turning their curved faces to the wall.

I hope you are saving these letters,
sons of mine

for Volume Four: "The Prison Letters
of Frankenstein's Unfortunate Mistake
who did not break under torture or
if he did he had his attention distracted
while they stitched him back together
to face more machines."

The title is long winded.
But then so is life.

Children. I am not even a poetry.
I am a philosoph.

Last night they bound and gagged me.
They rammed a voice into my ear
and they crooned that this
is to be my last letter.
They are holding my broken paws as I type.

I am muter than mute. As mute
as mute can be. Bloody mute.

Last night
they deprived me of my head
for sixty five days

and tied a starving prisoner
across my stomach
so that I could not dream.

A duck, my lads,
lying in weeds
miles from the land
months from the forest.

Closing the sunset gap
like a mouth

closed for the night.

SESSIONS

1.

It started with the telephone
ringing ringing
as I threw the baby down
(she bounced)
tripped over the push chair
(I bounced)
put my foot through the telly
(It's rented)
and I got there.
And it stopped.
And I turned.
And it started.
And I turned
and I grabbed the mouthpiece

and a voice said
            "Ian McWilliams?"
and I said

        "No but I could be"

and the voice said

       "I'm running a little festival"

       "Oh yes" I said.

       "At my little school in Thurton-on-the-Marsh"

       "Oh yes" I said.

       "I've got a mime artist. At least
       I think I have.
       He never answers the phone"

       "Oh yes"

       "I've got a theatre group.
       They're doing Shakespeare.
       Macbeth. Do you know Macbeth?"

       "Oh yes"

       "They're doing it in Eskimo Dress.
       Three witches as polar bears"

       "Oh yes"

       "And I thought
       well I thought
       yes I thought
       I ought to have
       some poetry."

She pronounced it Poyertroy.

       "Oh yes"

       "I wrote to Faber.
       And Faber.
       They were both out.
       But a really nice man
       agreed to send a blow up doll
       of Ted Hughes"

       "Oh yes"

       "And then I tried
       to get some other poets
       I tried

Roger McGough
Adrian Henri
Adrian Mitchell
Adrian Adrian
and finally
I got through
to you."

"Oh yes."

"Will you do it?
Will you do it?
I can pay you £40.00
plus travel.

Will you do it?"

"Okay.
I'll do it."

"Good. I've sorted out some trains.
You leave Barnsley at 0408
and you get to our school
just an hour before we start.

I'm so glad you can do it."

2.

The drunk
on the 5.am train
is poking his slopbucket breath
into my face.

"Now then pal,
what's your line of work?"

I stare into his eyes,
see the same face
I saw in the mirror
at four o'clock.

Normally I don't tell them.
Today I say
"I'm a poet".

The drunk
on the 5.am train
is poking his slopbucket breath
into my face.

"Poet? I know a poem:
Miranda dear Miranda
I love your little bum
specially when you sit it
on my big fat tum"

The train stops.
All the sleepy passengers
are staring at me.

And as he repeats the poem
twice, three times,
I feel my ticket
burn away in my pocket.

3.

Mr. McErrrr
I'd like you to meet Mr. Thrust;
He's a taxidermist-in-schools.
Mr. Thrust, Mr. McErrrr
He stuffs things, yes, for a living . . .
Isn't that amazing Mr. . . . .
We've read about these people who stuff things
and here's one in the flesh.
As it were.

What's in his bag?
You may well ask.
It's his badger.
It was flattened by a tractor.

He's going to stuff it
in lessons three and four
for a group of slow learners
in a temporary classroom

and we thought that
as he stuffed it
you could improvise a poem
like the troubadours used to.

You can do it Mr. Mc
You can do it.
I know you can.
You can do it.

4.

"Children . . . (I haven't told them you're coming. It's a surprise!
They *hate* poetry!) . . . Children . . . this gentleman is Mr., er, and do
you know what he does? No Darren, he isn't a pervert. No, Tracy, he
isn't a gorilla in a suit. No, he's a poet. He's had several books
published. He's been on Radio 3. He's met Peter Redgrove! He's
going to read you some of his poems, and then maybe get you to write
some. Isn't that exciting? Isn't it? Isn't it?"

PUSHING, MAY 1984

Kate's pink bonnet bobs
as she points to a flower.

I wheel her pushchair forward
she leans over to the colours.

Last time I brought her here
she was only two months old

and she never made a sound.
This time she shouts and points.

A tree moves, a car moves,
a striking pitman picks coal

shuffling the dirt, his dark head
bobbing. When we get back home

she won't have any words
to tell her mother what we saw

but she'll try. She starts to cry,
she always does when I turn her round

to push her back, her finger pointing.

„ Kate's Pink bonnet ..

PART FOUR

Poems by Shirley Bell

„ Sliced Manhattan „

LINCOLNSHIRE

This flat plate of landscape has been dished up
without devices. Land:sky, sky:land are
locked in endless blank exchanges where
the houses are pasted flat against the ground,
weathered by wind into the digesting soil,
as permanent as the Romans' salt pans.

The castle is already swallowed up
to a dry moat, choked with thirsty willows,
to the endless circling of shadows,
staring across a treeless estuary of mud
at the Church and the memory of the Abbey –
only lines on the land are left.

In the morning, it is all sky out there.
It takes eternity to see the stooping pullers,
bagging brassicas and cultivating invisibility.
This landscape's like chalked blackboards:
a careless sleeve, brushing past, would rub us out;
our lines like hares' breath, such tiny hieroglyphs.

STUBBLE-BURNING

Spilling hot beads across the field
I balanced the fire on a pitchfork
to shake it out, little by little.

Then it was animal, running from us,
quickly, quickly. Cracking our ears
with the sound of its feet, urgent

through the stubble. Where its black
prints showed the white smoke thinned,
darkened. And the sky obliterate.

You, too, running ahead of me. 'Think
what you're doing, lad!' Thickened air,
dancing with charred pepper. I would

consume . . . Next there was a slow grey
sky, something soft, with velvet
and violet in it. The stubble blued

and trailed with lines of ash. And in
the dusk white eyes of fire, blinking
at the smoke that stings to tears.

How you turned and said 'not you,
you're too . . .' You laughed. As if I
couldn't fail to understand. And yet

came spring, the corn half grown, my
tongue flickered on your body. Until
you burned, arching in the tractor ruts.

You asking 'have you met my bit of rough?'
Speculative eyes and laughter, my hands
and feet grown bigger. Something burning.

The sky consumed in black. I stayed behind
and watched the fires, transformed to
chains of party lights across the field.

NEXUS

This road as string, landmarks
twisting it to knots.

All the houses stay behind to
drown in saturated fields. Instead
pot-bellied cooling towers balance
on these stilts, and slop their
induced currents in the Trent.
Now tower blocks are straddling
entrances and exits: hanging
windows on the dark, the little
tapers held to say "we're here".
A TV mast blinks on and off,
strange legerdemain to conjure
disbelief with all its absences.

And in between balletic cartwheels,
then the cooling belly of the car.
Such a dark knot on these banal
fields, such an altered landscape.

BOMBER COUNTY

These curdled days, the nappies belly on the line.
She thins her eyes to watch the silver needles
darn the blue with such a delicate embroidery.
The noise comes after, cracking edge to edge
of this blank amphitheatre, dark bandage for the
baby's ears whose lips blow bubbles in his sleep.

The thin canopy is pierced by that slick armour.
Whipcrack sounds recross evacuated skies above
a chequerboard of winter wheat and yellow rape;
the houses strung like beads along the empty roads.
From there the sea is solid. Its corrugated jaws
have gnawed into the strategies of muddy coasts.

So drab a uniform to dress uneasy weeks. Near dawn
the windows flicker on and off, as practice bombers
intercept the quiet. The baby drowses, pale as milk,
and every day repeats a lullaby to rock his cradle to.

BEACHY HEAD

The sky is thin,
though it's so blue you'd think it solid ——.
It makes no promises to the heavy-footed.
The cliffs are pale and seamed:
at their feet, the sea is lace and bridal,
puckering and frilling.

The sea-birds trawl,
hollow-boned and buoyant. Their throats
make noises that demented women's do,
locked in geriatric wards.
The cliff tops are green plush, and smell of salt,
and, giddy, fall away.

The men are
grotesque wounded things, strapped in flapping lumber ——
they drag their gaudy rubbish on their backs.
Their sails glow,
boiled sweets; translucent sticky colours;
red and green and acid.

They run off cliffs
like grainy silent news-reels of those birdmen,
who windmilled heavy arms, and fell, and fell . . . ,
defy the dizzy drop
to plot their delicate draughtsmen's arcs,
and hang and glide.

CHAPEL SIX MARSHES

This is a hollow the tide has left. The water is pin-tucked;
again and again it pleats the same glittery fabric.
Animated pennies, round and brown as coppers,
the sandy crabs shadow-walk across the gathered bottom.
The starfish decorate a blank and astrological space ——
their warty arms waver where pale shrimps dart,
and soft pink things float like flesh, rubbery and indeterminate.
A big fist of crab whirs its excavator arms
and flails its clinking fingers down into the mud,
leaving a barnacled shell and two watchful eyes behind.

Across the Wash trees are a string of barges on the water-line.
Only the stubble-smoke finger points up to show its land ——
meeting then rolling below the warm froth of cloud cover.
You say it's called "anti-cyclonic gloom" – it sounds like mine.
Something dense and low, and arbitrary as the weather,
leaving two watchful eyes behind.

SLATE WORKS

In the mornings, his job stops
our windows. The hills wear masks –
tissues of bracken, horizontal
birches, darkened spruce.
But scratch their sides, and how
the paper fractures spill their bones!

Slate roofs and walls us;
fences fields of silly sheep
and us. Above our heads
blue gravestones rise in tiers
until they meet the purpled cliff.
One day we'll lie together under slate.

The dark hole heads our valley
where constant wind paws the foxgloves,
and the river's throat is stopped
with rock. Through the years
the quarried staircase has risen
on sheets of fine wafers; violet rows.

Lately, as he holds me to him,
I think I taste the mountain
on his lips. And in the darkness,
when he turns away, I watch him strike
a matchhead on his hardened palm.
Its small flame flickers, blue as slate.

OUT FOR SUNDAY TEA

It's only a bus ride –
then I'm back in that dusk-dark garden
where martins scream of leaving
the rowan berries splash the path.
My cousin and I are anyone we want.
There's the vinegar taste of salmon,
and the sweet geometry of fruit from tins.
The grown-ups talk and drink their tea
while our eyes prickle into roundness
in the darkening panes. "Pretend that I'm . . ."
But it's almost time to go.
At home, my uniform rustles in the wardrobe.
Stiff and uncompromising,
it knows better who I have to be.

I call back once.
My daughter walks the unfamiliar lawns
and watches her changing face
in a pond that wasn't there. "Sorry."
We didn't make the wedding and my cousin's gone.
My aunt displays a hanger; a white discarded dress.
I try to fill it out –
but she could be anyone if I met her now.
We grown-ups talk and drink our tea.

THE FAMILIAR EAVES

Spring, and the returning swallows
Scribble their remembered messages
Across the sky. Their programmed brains
Have sectored the empty air,
And mapped a course from Africa
To the customary tiles.
Each year they smear their mud huts
On these gutters.

This year the script is Gothic.
The swallows stutter in a German sky,
And trace their hesitating arcs
Above a catastrophic ash of bombing.
They cannot doubt the accurate cartography
Of skulls, or that they've homed correctly.
Roofless refugees, they haunt the skies,
Searching in vain for their familiar eaves.

THE BOATING LAKE

Here, in the darkness, I grin disjointedly
And subterranean currents pluck the lyre of my ribs.
Dark water ripples slowly through the spaces of my skull.
The air is a memory.
                    I disbelieve
The stream that dribbled prettily; a pocked lake surface
Where sugared blossom dripped in an artifice of acers;
A smack of oars, and a sky that slid away.
I danced clumsily as the water sieved me down.

Riddled, like a cheese, with old quarries,
The lake bed has a hidden geography.
Slow water fingers leach beneath the town.
My flesh has streamed away.
                    My emptied head
Rolls with the rhythmic surging of the flow.
I am an old tale to terrify the children.
On the lake the painted boats bob on the spangled water:
In the depths, I'm holding out my bony hands.

DOG-DAYS

Under the sun, today, the beach was
bone-white with emptied shells.
So many deaths. The sea growled
and threw foam anklets round
the children's legs: such silly
fetters to make them squeal and run.

Overhead, dark shuttles flew
above the caravans to a coast
where beaches falter into marsh.
Then practice bombs thudded through
the afternoon, like heartbeats.

Now the tide is turning,
and candied lights glisten
on the river mud: cinema neon,
tungsten filament, traffic signals,
clicking – red, amber, green;
the cars pulsing through the night.

In a sky as deep as history,
Sirius winks one bright eye,
sleepless. These are dog-days:
thickening with heat,
and filled with waiting.

RAPUNZEL

I live in this smooth "o".
Which has no entrance
but the window and
the ladder of my yellow hair.
My mouth opens: how I sing!

In here it's dark and secret,
red plush, such a warm hollow.
Your face turns towards
my subtle chant; these walls,
and how to scale them?

The sorceress runs upwards,
spider-wise. The thread quivers.
There are doors which you must open.
Your thoughts harden on my
snug interiors, blind caves.

Now you must call and enter:
"Your hair, Rapunzel." But
she has my place, tops the shaft.
The bird is flown, and the cat
will have the best of you.

You'll fumble for my music.
Soon, I will see you blind
and heal you with my tears.

THE MERMAID

Always I would be in air –
the green rim tilting to
a gasp, then fractured sun
and the comb, moving
through my briny hair.

I led you, dry-limbed,
to a place of bones. When
pity pressed my mouth
on your drowning lips,
you woke to my sea music.

My salty kisses silenced you.
Then our children mewed
like gulls. Your eyes were
always filled with something
stirring, deep as water.

Soon my salt notes stung
your ears. Now your eyes
are emptied like the sky,
and my sisters' voices call
in the chuckle of the swell.

The sea draws nearer. You are
a dry whisper. In dreams
the water closes on my head
and fills my lungs like peace.
These days I walk on knives.

WHODUNNIT

Detective Inspector Clench crouches
at his dinner.
His wife is hostage;
pastes herself against the wall
and tries to slide into the kitchen
before the shouting starts.

Clench has seen it all.

Children with closed eyes,
battered men,
and the old ladies with purpling faces.
Torn clothes. A single shoe.
That mummified baby,
tucked in a shawl of old newspapers:
Daily Herald, 1933.
And a white-faced Miss
who claimed she didn't understand.

Clench chews his meat
tasting human debris, long pig.
He sucks the bones
and thinks about anatomy –
the meticulous superstructure,
a white scaffolding
that the dogs dig up.
You'd think it had been bleached.

His dreams are larded
with the whispered pleas of victims:
nos, and stops, like chunks of fat.

His villains seem so ordinary.
They comb their hair and brush their teeth,
their shoes are polished.
Some read Shakespearian sonnets,
and like to see live theatre.
At times Clench offers cigarettes
and laughs with them.

But in the night
a strangler's iron hand
fingers his heart.
It's then he feels that he's the victim really,
and asks himself whodunnit.

A CARTOGRAPHER'S ANNIVERSARY

Twelve chartless years
sheeted in bridal mists, making maps.

Seas like polished mirrors.
Taking soundings on the breathing swell,
licking the spindrift salt
of rocks that come and go;
slick seals' heads laced in foam.
Voyages round your granite definitions,
the veiled obsidian face, reflective:
my ragged coasts and briny estuaries.
Bone islands. Land bridges.

Expeditions to the lush interior,
where tongues twist, sense fails:
we make translations.

This is a love story:
now the maps are drawn.

THE BODY BOOK

My child is two and talks to me:
'The shell-head in my body'. He means
his skull, tucked tight and white.

'Bang your head, you'll feel it.' Now
he laughs to hear his fingers drum.

And though I join him, I can hear
the sound of salt-fresh water running
out, out, out, leaving weary nothings.

Tide-wrack and this heavy, silted head.

SEA-SIDE

I

The dunes wear a mohair of grass,
a lurex of silvery buckthorn,
while the squat conifers crouch darkly
with their arms full of new spring candles.
Around the wheels of the car
buttercups lift their pallid faces.
I watch a starling stuffing its importuning youngster
with indiscriminate gobs of grubs.
The fledgling totters and flaps its wings,
and gapes its beak for more, more, more . . .

II

Back over the sea-wall, the wind slaps my face.
The sea is crumpled tin-foil
spread across the dull metal beach
with its patina of pebbles.
Wigs of seaweed lie about
amongst the pebbles' bony crunch,
and the stupid noses of the paper cups.
My daughter, pink skirt flapping,
balances on the dark finger of the breakwater;
watches the water bubbling in,
stirring tesserae of grit in the dimpled sand.
She has found a rock striped like a tiger,
and a stone which glows like a ruby.
She cries like a bird, "Come and see. Come and see."
My small son winces over the shingle
dragging an encrusted crow-bar of wood.
"Look, look, stick," he says.
The baby waves his arms at me
and opens his clamorous gape.

WET-BOB

This is a wide-hulled ship, cargo-laden.
It palpitates with shifting darknesses
And its engorged belly heaves and swells.
Inside the hollow land, time is tidal,
Measured by an oar-stroke of heartbeats,
While jerkily your star-fish hands and splayed feet
Test out their watery boundaries,
And your frondy fingers quiver like anemones.

Lulled and lapped and dammed within the hulk,
Its inner shores relentlessly contracting,
I wonder if you know a storm will brew?
When these peaceful harbour-walls turn outside-in
You must make headway, and your frail craft prepare to meet
The white light, shocks, and the metallic clankings
Of an arbitrary and dry-footed world.

SOFT FRUITS

In the city, the sky was fitted
in the space between the roofs:
that summer it was a blue jigsaw,
interrupted by clouds, and starlings
coming in to roost. One sticky night
we said we'd go and earn a tan. But
I wasn't ready for the hot weight
on my back; that sun filled press,
squeezing the flattened parallel
of fields tramlined into 'v's
with strawberries. The perfumed air
was sick with them and so was I.

In the tent we'd lie and count the
bumping shadows coming from the pub.
His fingers on my body smelt of
strawberries, strawberries on his lips,
his tongue. Such a short season before
I fled, and left behind the rows
of bloody noses, clotted on the green.

EEL-FARE

River threads into sea, swallowed tidally:
to reappear tide-washed, puckering across the sand,
the endless skeins winding, winding. There is
a light here, brimming with characteristic reflections
and significance sharp as needles or the cutglass voices
of us children. Interrupting eel-fare. You have to learn
to see them, ripples in the rippled sand, water clear
with press-stud eyes, pouring into buckets.

Elvers in oil; they coil like vermicelli on the plates.
'This kind of pallid food looks best
in earthenware.'
We tipped the buckets out.

Those were children, calling on a Cornish beach,
where the sand was punctuated with rocks. Stippled with
hair hanks, green and red and brown,
bearing little bladders that exploded
to a screwing fingertip. I was nine, with a shorn round bob.
Now Ali threads his fingers through my hair:
"A big treatment, yes?"
Henna and curls, my lipstick mouth's ritual movements.
And the car, too, moving through a grid of drains
and dykes, where oil-dark water sulks with eels.

How can they come so far – Sargasso Seasfull
of them to slime and stretch through crannies in the rocks
and grow their yellow bellies: olive slugs
in sluggish olive water?
And yearn across the wetted grass to shallow ponds
where herons paddle and their eel-ropes wind and wind.

ERZULIE

Loosely, I'm Erzulie: ruby-faceted
triple-ringer for the black Venus.
How perfumed! Watch the dipping
of my hips. I'm lavish though
three husbands fetter me. Look.
I'm a bagfull of satiations;
a pouch for others' sorrows.

My first husband flickers from me,
pale as tapers, white as candle-fat.
His eyes are stained blue windows
where nothing moves but clouds, and
the slow wings of one perfected bird.
Echoes fill his stone house. Now
his cold mouth moves on pebbles.

My second husband says:–
"Bleed me your sons, I can use them
row on row as sandbags for my walls.
You are the one who must look on with
little frightened faces tucked into
your arms. I pluck strange blossoms,
crimson flowers to bloom upon your hem."

I am Erzulie, who has to weep for love
that turns to stones, to bones; for
all the substances less durable than
finger-rings. Meet my third husband:
I will crumble in these arms. See his
morning suit, my veils; flowers whose
incense shrouds us in the darkened car.

This is the one true bridegroom. Who'll
hold me in the last and best embrace.
Until as dust I rise upon his breath.

(ERZULIE – goddess of love in the Voodoo pantheon; married
   simultaneously to the ascetic, the warrior, and death)

AFTERBIRTH

Here is a new blurred body:
it has breathed you out
of its puckered belly.
Such fine blue veins
criss and cross
the Danish cheeses of its breasts
which harden into generosity.
When you waken from your secret sleep
your eyes are milky as your lips.
Purr for your cream, now,
my little cat.

The lake has trapped a swan

PART FIVE

Poems by John Turner

On cold Barry Beach..

HAPPY RETURNS

The conquering hero comes home
From the Falklands
From the sea he comes
From the shells and the mortars.
The conquering hero comes home
To Park Street
To banners he comes
To bunting and streamers
To Connie he comes
And a wide red flag
And a cheering crowd
Shouting
Welcome home Dennis
Home from the war
A home fit for heroes
A home for the free.

But also in Park Street
Higher in Park Street
Is Sharon relocated
From James Street
Sharon waving a wide red flag
And a boy and a girl
Shouting
Welcome home Dennis
Home from the war
The home where we're waiting
Patiently.

The conquering hero turns back
From the cheering
Turns back from the welcome,
The flags and the bunting.
The conquering hero crumples
His four-day pass
Boards the train
Travelling back to the depot
Travels back to the mess-room
To stories of glory
To whisky and gin.

AN EXCURSION

In this light
It is difficult to tell
Exactly where we are.
It may be Grantham
Put away for the night;
It may be Peterborough
Where rainwater muddies the platform.

Chris totters down the carriage
With three beer cans.
A mime artist
Shouts in the buffet.
Pete is asleep.

The man in the neat suit
Speaks softly
Of the men he has killed
In Africa.
A nuclear bomb
Dropped now on Newark
He whispers
Would atomise the train in an instant.

The train rocks,
The man in the neat suit falls silent –
Already he has revealed too much.

Jammed up tight in the second class
In this night
It is difficult to tell
Exactly where we are.

SUNDAY AFTERNOON

The Galactic
Storm-trooper
Stalks the rebels.
Perchow! Perchow!
Blasters speak.
The small leader
Crawls along the wall
In low profile.

Mr. Babbage
Washes his car,
Strangely immune
To blaster fire;
Hears shouts
From the bushes:
'I'm not dead
You missed me.'

Mr. Babbage
Places an
Arthritic grip
On the hose-pipe,
Takes painful aim,
Hits the nearside wing
With a thud of water
At point-blank range;
Mutters with purpose
I'm not dead.
You missed me.

KNUCKLEDUSTERS IN THE PARK

The boy
Displayed like a school prize
In his crisp brown blazer,
Walks happily through the park
On his way to afternoon school.
He would be whistling
But he hasn't yet learned how.
Someday he will practise for a few hours
And master the art.
Until then
The sun is shining,
The park is warm and friendly.
The boy is rehearsing
The new language
He has just developed.
Trahez Cèl Portia Jual Lors
He muses
Refining
A small point of grammar.

Suddenly
He hears a different tongue.
A voice snaps
Oi
You go to Bradford Grammar School?
The boy
Answers innocently
Yes.

A large fist appears
From nowhere.
Knuckledusters
Come down hard
Into a youthful head,
Biting,
Crunching,
Explosive sound.

A knuckleduster blow to the skull
Is a sharper pain in the temple
Than an afternoon of algebra.

For the next few days
The boy walks uneasily
Through the park.
He wears his father's glasses
And a Trilby hat,
A blotchy moustache
Drawn above his upper lip
With shoe polish.

The detective says –
Keep walking through the park lad,
If he has a go at you again,
We'll nab him.

The boy
Is unimpressed
With this aspect
Of police-work.

TECHNOLOGY

It's not easy to identify when
The festive carousings turned to fisticups.
At least there would be difficulty
But for Video Reflections Limited.
(Give yourself a lasting memory of
The most precious day of your life.)

The sergeant yawns through white Rolls Royces,
Through simpering girls in velvet frocks,
Through cocky youths in cheap new suits,
Through squawking laughter and doubtful toasts.
Sits up in interest as glasses break,
As bar stools somersault, as bouquets fly.

Hits the rewind button
Freezes frame
Consults a colleague
Makes rapid notes.
Watches
The Wedding Guests, caught motionless
Like blurred statues, at the groom's expense
Immortalised as Exhibit A.

MARSHLANDS

It was the night of the great fire
Kindled bright to roast the carcass
The flesh searing spitting bubbling
The scent of burning sycamore
A heady incense to fuel dreams.
I followed him from the clearing
While others danced
While others chanted.
I am by right my father's heir
Mine the silver spear and shield
I drove my knife into his heart
I watched my brother fall and die
While others danced
While others laughed.
But one reveller had slipped away
Shadowed me quietly through the night
Observed me in the bloody deed
While others laughed
While others drank.

In the morning of the North Light
I was roughly roused and led away
Thrown down and forced onto my knees
A cord of cow-hide around my neck
The choking tightening of my throat
Awful embracing of present death
My body slapped into the shallow pool
While others slept
While others dreamed.

In a distant gloomy morning
I am gently hauled up from the past.
A foreign clan of men and women
Clean my body, lay me on muslin
Remove the cord with quiet whispers
Pluck hairs out from my ginger beard
Soft flabby hands arrange my limbs
Much chattering and talk in tongues
I cannot really quite make out.

There are no hunters in this tribe
No holy men, no strong chieftains
No guards to warn of sudden attack
I have not seen a running deer.
There is no spirit in those here
The strange attraction to one man's death
Six days circling round an ancient corpse.
This is not the way to end my days
While others sleep
While others forget.

A1 RUNNER

Cutting easily
Through Cambridgeshire
In the dark
A snowstorm of cornflies
In my headlights
Splatter, splash
Against my windscreen.
Shall I move into the back
Leave the car
To drive itself.
I have little enough say
In any journey
They are all mapped out.

Just down from
The roundabout
A man in
Shirt-sleeves
Runs from his
Empty car
On the grass verge
Doors flung open
Bags strewn on the ground.
Tests himself
Against the miles
Feet thumping
On the earth
Will wrestle hard

With every pace
Will feel the moist air of the wood
Will feel the turf yield
Beneath his footfall.

Go back round the roundabout
Wind the gear back through one turn
Freeze the man in his mad run
Stop him dead in his mid-stride
Drive round again to wind the gear
Another turn to turn the man

Winch him back into his car
Back into the driving seat
Hands gripped on the steering wheel
Doors slammed shut, the engine on
See the car drive off again.

Cut easily through
Cambridgeshire
Reclining through the miles.

LISTER'S MILL, BRADFORD

1) *Schooldays*

Quarter past seven
My father brings my morning cup of tea –
Switches on the extension speaker
From the wireless downstairs.
Jack de Manio announces the wrong time.
My father draws back the curtains
And smiles inquisitively.
Sometimes I think he is about to kiss me
But it would not do.
Once I made as if to hug him
Clumsily.
I pretended I had lost my balance
He gave me half a crown.

Quarter to eight
Jack de Manio talks to a boy
Who is incubating a parrot's egg
Under his armpit.
I look through my window.
Sometimes I wake to sunlight.
Not today.
Lister's Mills' furnaces are fully charged;
Dense curtains of black smoke
Hide the sky
Offer me a sooty greeting.
Lister's Mill Chimney
Fills my window –
As tall as Blackpool Tower
Wider than two houses.
It is well-known
That the parapet on the chimney-top
Is so wide
That two coaches and horses
Can be driven around it
Abreast.

Quarter past eight
Jack de Manio explains that the studio clock
Is difficult to see from his chair.
I dress.
Mother gives me Quaker Oats
Longs to escape to clearer air
Far from the dirt and grime
The chimney spews out.

It's a re-assuring sight for all that.
When, as a younger boy,
I would go on long walks with my parents
On Baildon Moor,
Exhausted, cold, almost crying
I would see it
On the distant skyline
Tall, black against the sky
Beckoning me home.

Half past eight
I leave for school.
Dan Woodend opens up his butcher's shop
Pauses as he unlocks the door
Glances upwards to the chimney top –
Wonders how they lifted the
Coaches and horses up.
Jack de Manio does not know.

2) *Adolescent*

The Mill's got
Beamsley Road
Cornered.
Not that it matters.
There's nowhere to go
Except the weaving sheds.

In the afternoon
I hang around B-Shed gate
To show off.
Auntie Elsie is the first
Hot from the looms
Fresh from their thrashing din.
I wave
She smiles.
Cousin Audrey next
Hair rolled tight
In curlers
Inside her headscarf.
Does not dignify the
Working day
With lipstick.
Auntie Nellie
In her cheery way
Passes by.
I'm the bright boy
In the family
Always take care
To use long words.

My mother
Sometimes suspect
The rest think her
Stuck-up
Because
She married a teacher
And once
Went to Belgium
On holiday.

Cousin Jean tells me
That Grandma
Is worse again.
I nod sadly.
It's expected.
I'm not really listening.

We have a different
Batch number.
You in your small corner
I in mine.

3) *Holiday Job*

Not the grimy walls outside
But the men within.
Men who hide
Among the wool bins.
It's a living of sorts
At least it's life.
Bitter memories
Of Warsaw
Or the Ukraine
Can still sting
Life a knife.
Dimitri and Bolek
Look up from their chess game
And wink.
I push my skip
Of knitting wool
Along the shed
And mark the stock card.

4) *Summer Visitors*

Emilia listens patiently
As I reminisce.
The first visit
We've made together
To my home town,
Sitting on a wall
Directly underneath
The chimney
Craning our necks
To see it's top.
The busy terraces
That crowded round
Are gone.
The mill stands apart –
Fires put out
Stonework cleaned
Gleaming
Looking for all
Like a Florentine Palace
In a deserted Piazza Vecchio.

5) *Iconoclast*

Brian
In his quiet way
Has the answers
Spearing
A sly tortilla
In the restaurant.
He has the ear
Of the public records officer
Knows the secret
Suppressed for years
Has seen the plans,
Measured the drawings.
The parapet
On the Chimney Top
Is three foot six wide.
Two dogs could not
Run round abreast.

Dan Woodend at 72
Would not survive the shock
Of this unwelcome truth.
I
At half that age
Merely choke on my coffee.

THE HEART OF THE MATTER

On cold Barry Beach
Four men
Sit shivering
In a caravan
Talking poetry;
The wind
Rocking us
Like a schooner
Tossed in rough seas.
The posh one has written
Over two hundred poems
(But left them at home).
The noisy one
Once sat next
To Dylan Thomas
(In a bar).

The Tall one asks
My opinion of Auden
As we trudge along
The beach car park
Returning from
The Urinal
(Twyfords).
I notice
That all of us
Have splashmarks
(On our shoes).

A type tossed up a Lamppost

PART SIX

Poems by David Harmer

„a black and white dog …

PICKETS WALKING THROUGH A FIELD: JANUARY

Snow. Iron framed fields,
rigid earthworks fixed in ice.

Every morning passing through
corroded farmland
they bunch their fingers round their mouths
like bruises.

Trees jab a bed of nails
into the morning, eyesight hardens
staring out the cold.

The air bites back,
beats on unprotected heads.
Networks delicate as cobwebs
tumble down a young man's face.

They rub their hands against his blood,
feel his laughter spilling out
in large red clumps

clustered on the muddy track
like poppies.

ARRAS

He showed me the post,
a white exclamation
stopped with poppies.

The woods vibrate,
sweat prickles our collars
sticking our palms to polished metal.
The paths are dry
slightly stirred by tyre-tracks.

"They shot them here," he said.
"Just outside the city walls."

My hands are bleeding,
chafed at the wrists they stain
the dust shrouding my boots.

Zeros confront us,
stacked in ranks, mouths open.
Tongues protrude
with schoolboy concentration.
Their eyes tighten.

In quivering light mosquitoes
flick the skin from their wings.

MEETING IN OCTOBER

Our conversation yesterday
rolled over my head

like water, huge green pools
half-covered in leaves and floating
reeds

rolled over the mallard
we fed one autumn day in London.

My feet ached. You snapped
pigeons as they scaled my face,
later

ducks scratched faint parallels
across the negative.
St. James' Park

towards the evening
half-lit water, the smell of bonfires.

I found I was
completely surrounded by birds.

Huge brown geese,
swans with necks the thickness
and breadth of a wrestler's
forearm

stabbed the bread I offered.

No sanctuary
amongst the wings, feathers, beaks.
The wind twisted

leaves, exposed pale undersides
whiter than the swans.

THE WHITBY ROAD

A humped bridge anticipates
that long descent to bleached hotels
curved and stiff as whalebone.

The rooftops squabble
for land that always was uncertain,
each yard a bargain
argued out with stubborn contours.

Seabirds haze the harbour,
they scream aloud like drowning men
harpoons spent, their nets broken.

SEARCHING FOR DRACULA

In the harbour
flocks of trawlers bunch
against the cold.

Above the houses, jostling
like frightened peasants

a woman roots amongst the dead.

The sky has wings
flattened back to meet the storm.
It circles the wind-pocked graves.

Her church is a ship
emptied of crew by an undead cargo
stalking for blood.

She has been told
the grave is not here,
eroded angels explained

but the wind flung their words
to the gulls.

ONE AFTERNOON

We climbed a tower
timber-built and reaching
high into November

the air chilled blue, each lung
a branch weighed down with cold.

The forest crouched,
suggested movements pencilled
near the trunks. The sky

sprang at us so fresh and clear
we swore to seeing dolphin tracks
cut through it.

All of us caught above the snowline.
It was so deep that we abandoned
both cars and trudges

almost up to our thighs
just off the highway, south of Vermont.

GARDENING WITH MY FATHER

Our weight combines
to lean against the tree
a storm has badly twisted.

He pushes hard enough for me
to wedge the base
then tug a knotted rope around
a neighbour's fence.

Bending down I shovel earth
against the roots, a branch
whips against my palm
driving splinters through the skin.

I look at him but realise
these days my hands are my affair.

TWO CIRCLES: IRONBRIDGE GORGE

Two circles.

An iron bridge.

A stone moon.

The river carves steep rocks,
limestone slabs thick with trees.

Behind our shoulders
houses scramble up the hillside
on bare feet.

They reach the clear
blue evening, raise their branches.

Cup their hands to take the weight
of rookeries. Each window
reflects two circles.

The river curves,
a dark green mirror
thick with clay and sand.

The bridge drowns.

The moon sinks.

GULLS

Strong winds diminish these birds,
toss scraps of land to their grasping claws
then fling them back to sea.

Fishermen drowned in the hump-backed waves
watch the sky darken with wreckage.

Their trawlers scurry towards
a dark grey line scratched into slate
as thin as the edge of the world.

ARKENGARTHDALE

Acres grown against the grain
hammer down the long horizons.

These farms harvest stone, forced
up in slabs like graveyard lumber.

A tractor stumbles, drags
the gradient beneath its wheels

and streams abandon all pretence
of water.

To penetrate this country
you must crawl, slide into darkness

worm and tunnel through its skull,
crop the roots of thrusting rock.

SWINSIDE STONES: CUMBRIA

A curlew bickered
over the rain, scolded and scattered

droves of sheep stamped flat
on the hillside.

Inside the circle
a small child tottered,
uncertain of weight or position.

The stones stretched out to touch her,
hunching their cowls against the weather.

They murmured and whispered
rumours concerning the tide and sand
shifting the estuary we could glimpse
between their cracked shoulders.

Outside I splashed
up to my ankles in long wet grass,
scampering widdershins

to summon rain and angry birds
that circled the child,
whose weight we took on our shoulders.

RUMOURS FROM THE BISHOP'S ESTATE

The land lies flat on its back,
waits for sunlight to burn it yellow.

Cottages gather round the river's curve.

Cobbled by rock, slabs of water
carry the village to where a church

squats inside its hollow,
a toad trapped beneath damp stone.

At evening, graveside poplars
shuffle through the jostling dead
clustered round each door.

The toad croaks,
swallows one more fly.

● ● ●

Wood drives wood
to power stone, water heaves
against the grain.
The gearing mutters,
an engineering carved out of hills.
Cogs shiver in the dark,
stuffing their guts with corn.

● ● ●

The breeze hums a shanty
home from the sea. Tops of trees
murmer politely.

The fields glitter with harvest.

Mills bend their backs
to buckle and strap
whole winds to their purpose.

Grind down. Reduce. Pulver.

Villagers blister, heat and grit
rub callouses into their hands

shackled together each Sunday.

SLAGHTMAAND

Snow is coming.

An ice whisper
rattles in the sky's voices.

The horizon glitters,
a knifeblade slitting open
black throated hills, the moorland's belly

bleeds dark water, peat bogs
and rough pastures
will soon be salted down

preserved until the thaw.

Our boats are numbed,
timbers drenched and soaked
the keels scraped across the beach.

Their carcasses are gutted,
they overturn, exposing open wounds.

Soon the sky will be butchered.

The beasts always know our coming.
They raise their blunt muzzles
dripping from the mud

watch the axes
like the children watched us
carve and hack their village
this time last year.

Now our boats are beached,
drying out their bones.

Once more a year sinks to its knees
bellows out a death,
our axes cut deep red lines
through the sky's neck

at the time of slaughter
a month before winter comes.

PEPYS AT THE TOWER

Eventually I would not dig
but sat beside a raging fire
(it being December and lately snowed)
reading plays.

In the garden my companions
hacked the leather-hardened clay
for firkins stuffed with gold.

To small avail, there was no treasure
although the codes were old and cracked
and every attic visited.

Enough of folly, I shall write
newly-minted ciphers,
sit beside my good red fire
and bury firkins of my own;

let others dig who may.

SUBSIDENCE

Thrusting her hand between
spreading cracks stuck to the walls
tougher than ivy, she laughs

then runs to the garden,
husband she cries, help me quickly
my clothes are on fire, I am burning.

Beneath the house foundations move,
gradually the earth dislodges
where the roof points out the sky.

She walks to the trees
holds long debates with the milkman
far into the dawn. She cries.

All the forms are completed,
damages assessed.

My bed is hard she cries
the sheets too white, I am burning
husband, burning with the cold.

114

A PHONE CALL FROM ATLANTIS

The voices are distant, limpets
spread their stomachs over the cables.

A sailor slid beneath the grease
scudding across Portsmouth harbour

slotted his coin
between the deck and the quay.

Bloated with achievement
he navigates new courses, steers
by the stars and takes on board

dockside shrimps pink as thumbs,
gouging open lips and eyes.

Again he turns, floats amongst
ruined buildings, broken columns.

He fills his pipe with sand.

Repeat caller
your last message, push
more coins into the slot.

Fingers burst, struck tight
inside the numbered metal rings

they explode, flesh floating
small ballons
through the thick green air.

CLIMBING BREEDON

To begin with a pebble
gagged my tongue. I sucked again,
tried to draw water from stone.

A child on his hands and knees,
I followed my mother
scrambling up a rutted track
through the hottest day that summer.

The fields grew harsher,
flies attacked cattle.
Gorged on dung they drowned
in the succulent eyes.

Because they brought no water,
the hill not steep, the day
a pleasant stroll through 1961

a penny was crammed
between my lips
by my parents to fetch up spit.

The sour metal stung my mouth
the coin was too cheap, too base
to buy off the world scorching my feet

as I choked on the lumps of it
forced down my throat.

WINTERBOURNE HALL

The wind's skeleton haunts the fields
flung round our path like broken stone.

Puddles splinter, shot through with mud
streaked with blue-veined marble.

A small wood crouches by the fence,
an ivory graveyard crammed
with wooden tusks and freezing bodies.

Hidden streams direct our path
towards the lake
a dull silver scratched by birds

reflects our breath in whispers.

● ● ●

Hold a mirror to this house.
Windows shatter, cut like ice
by skaters on a winter pond.

There is no cloud.

Inside each room our breathing
exhales the dust from sour museums,
floorboards creak above.

There are no footsteps.

Just the flow of conversations
several centuries old.
Beside the shining coffins
we mist the glass with words

● ● ●

The lake has trapped a swan,
feathers fused, beak snapping.

Its legs crack like the boards
of wooden ships explorers locked
in distant ice-fields.

The scream uncoils
along the neck arched with pain

as our pathway home
squirms out of sight into the fog

towards the lights
flung like curses across the evening.

BLACK AND WHITE MOVIE: 1964

At the studio gate
security guards allow his Buick
to pass unchecked. Why yes.
Certainly Mister. Sure.

Up to my chest in filthy water
with fat technicians pumping mist
over those slippery boards,
I will get shot in the harbour.

On location I'll pack a bottle,
drive to the shore. Two women
pass the Buick. Stare straight in.
Why yes. That face. Isn't it? You're.

At home he's a slob Alice,
Alice I swear. A real jerk-off.
Sits all day doing nothing for me,
saying nothing. A stinking bore.

Sunrise and sand upset the lighting,
his wife calls him up
don't come home any more.
In bed, on location, he checks his script.

This is me, my Buick, my skin
my blood. Eyes, hair, teeth, jaw.
Why yes. It is. Certainly. Sure.

THREE POEMS FOR LIZZIE

Dappled by shadows
my daughter
grasps a leaf
with her wrinkled fist.

She looks up,
puzzled by the sudden snap
as the leaf's green palm
crumbles.

118

Behind her green
and smoky stare
wild orchards tumble.

———

Lizzie and I blow bubbles
for each other.

She simply spits,
I need plastic rings and soap
to provide my floorshow.

She cannot speak to me
of how her finger stabs
each bloom

until our greasy, bouncing colours
vanish with a gasp.

———

The imprint of her body
is warm and small
on my shoulder.

Her head twists,
plunges into sleep again.

And I suppose

somewhere a child
pushes his small weight against
his father's shoulders.

One day they will dance together
each guiding the other's weight

making the imprint
of their baby.

PUB THEATRE: THE MILE END ROAD

Last night the wallpaper
grew hysterical
our jokes were so quick.

The mile ends here,
nobody pushes around this pub

where jukebox tunes
stagger through a lurching crowd.

The drunk who heckled
flings away his safety net
and stumbles on a reckless tightrope.

He begins to sob and sing
spilling every note.

The landlord smiles his knife tricks,
throwing back a giant head
he bounces laughter from the mirrors.

Upstairs his giant dog rolls over
to expose its belly,
no killer after all, a secret
we are begged to keep.

We are the secret here,
near the river, east of Whitechapel.

No-one bothers to disturb us;
we send the beerstained paper
wild with slick routines.

CERTAIN ASPECTS OF YORKSHIRE FOLKLORE

Above Robin Hood's Bay that night
rain cut their faces, rubbed salt
in their eyes as they hauled the boat
across open moorland, thrust
it down the crooked hill's throat
towards the shore where wreckage gathered
like sailors' widows.

Villages trapped by fire each morning
tighten their fingers.

Muscles bursting, bunched like horses
huge at the shoulder, a dozen men
slammed their bodyweight into the sea
drove the lifeboat in one clean line
straight through the current.
Waves smashed over its bows,
the oars engaged heaving water.

Drowned. Sucked down in one bite,
disgorged in splinters.
The sea's anger chocked the beach.

Villages harden
to long ropes of Whitby jet.
Featherstone, Fitzwilliam,
a hundred others.
They slam their bodyweight each day
into a lifetime's task of thrusting

lifeboats straight at an angry sea.

„ Clench chews his meat "

BIOGRAPHICAL NOTES

David Horner:
Born 1946, Hull. Graduated from Cambridge and lectured and taught in Sri Lanka and Austria. Currently teaching English in Warrington. Poems in a number of magazines in this country and abroad.

Martyn Wiley:
Born 1954, Barnsley. Writing poetry since 1977. Member of Versewagon Mobile Writing Workshop and Circus of Poets poetry/ cabaret group. Publications include *Just Like Eddie* (Stride 1983) and *The Country Sundays* (Littlewood Press 1985).

Ian McMillan:
Born 1956, Barnsley. Freelance Writer. Member of Versewagon and Circus of Poets. Four previous collections of poetry, most recent being *Now it can be told* (Carcanet 1983) and *How the Hornpipe Failed* (Rivelin Grapheme 1984).

Shirley Bell:
Born 1950, Birmingham. Now living on a Lincolnshire cactus farm with her physicist husband. She has a daughter, two small sons, and an Open University First in English/Art History. Her poems have been accepted for *NEW POETRY 8* and numerous magazines including Argo, Other Poetry, and Poetry Durham. Her work has also been broadcast on Radio 3's Poetry Now, and a selection of her poetry appears in Faber & Faber's *POETRY INTRODUCTION 6*.

John Turner:
Born 1948, Bradford. Member of Versewagon and Circus of Poets. Has worked as a teacher and Arts administrator. Previous collection: *Hard Shoulders Second Home* (Versewagon Press 1983).

David Harmer:
Born 1952. Member of Versewagon and Circus of Poets. Currently working as a teacher. Previous collection: *The Spinner's Final Over* (Versewagon Press 1983).

AFTERWORD

VERSEWAGON: PAST, PRESENT AND FUTURE

By the Spring of 1982, although I had been calling myself a freelance writer for over a year, I was finding that the only way I could make a living was by running Writing Workshops. As a result, I was involved with workshops all over South Yorkshire: Maltby, Rawmarsh, Wath, Barnsley, Mexborough. My experience was that workshops were fairly easy to set up, although they were difficult to keep going, and that the unusual or non-literary venue worked just as well as the obvious one. In other words, the workshop at Mexborough Citizens Advice Bureau went as well as the one at Maltby Library.

As a result of this I began to evolve an idea, with the people I was writing with at the time (John Turner and Martyn Wiley), of a mobile writing workshop. It would be a bit like the old peripatetic music teacher visiting a different school each day; we could visit a number of locations on a rota basis. It seemed like a good idea. We were trying to move away from the idea of workshops where you'd expect to find them, and into the idea of workshops in rural areas.

Then John's mate Ernie loaned him a VW Caravette. John came round to our house to work on our play; he showed me the caravette. "This would be good for the mobile writers' workshop" he said, meaning that it would be a good idea to travel to the workshop in the caravette rather than in someone's car. I thought he meant it would be a good idea to hold the workshop in the caravette; that would get rid of the need to book rooms, liase key-jangling caretakers and so on. It's that rare example of an idea born through not listening properly.

After a false start with a rusty wagon which fell to bits, we got hold of Ernie's wagon on a permanent basis, fitted it out with a central table and some lettering on the side, and Versewagon was on the road. We called it Versewagon because it was a Volkswagen and we were hoping for sponsorship from them. We're still hoping.

So, from the Summer of 1982 the pattern of the Versewagon day was established as we trundled up and down the country to Festivals, Arts Days, Book Fairs and markets. We'd arrive at the venue at about half-past nine in the morning and set up our bookstall, which was full of small press publications including pamphlets published by our own Versewagon Press. This bookstall was often a great help to people who weren't quite sure that they really wanted to bring their work to us. They could sidle up to the stall and pretend to peruse it as they glanced at us and worked out that we weren't mad. Or that we were mad. Part of our attraction, I am sure, is that we offer endless free coffee; people would often stay with us all day, drinking cup after cup. About ten to

125

ten the first customer would arrive, either sidling as described, or striding confidently with a neat file of work. And then we'd be at it all day, sometimes chatting on a one-to-one basis, sometimes having a readaround or group workshop if there were enough people. Always we emphasised practicalities, depending on what stage people were at: send your work to this magazine, not that one; type your work; read this poet, that novelist; get writers into your school; start your own writers workshop, your own magazine. We gave people handouts: how to set up a workshop, where to send work, how to present it and so on. The work blossomed and many highlights spring to mind: our day in March (the town not the Month) in Cambridgeshire, with our biggest crowd ever, almost thirty people throughout the day; our day in Telford, sharing the venue with a convention of drum majorettes and a model steam engine rally; four days in the Co-op car park in Cambridge, as the World's First Writers in Residence in a Co-op Car Park.

As time went on the idea of the one-off Versewagon day became modified; we worked in people's houses, in schools, in Libraries. Versewagon's expertise and personnel are now used as much as the Versewagon itself, which is how it should be. And of course the main advantage is meeting lots of very good writers: Shirley Bell in Boston, David Horner in Warrington, Diana Withington in Sheffield, Beth Edge in Barnsley, Chris Mills in Cardiff, John Desmond in March. It's a long list; there are writers everywhere, except Potters Bar, where nobody turned up, but that's a different story.

As to the future? Well, we'd like to get a new wagon; the present one is limping along but it won't last forever. We'd like to be used on more than a one-off basis, perhaps a series of visits to one locality over a year or two; we'd like to develop our schools work, and we'd like to go to places nobody would ever think of going to.

We'd even like to go back to Potters Bar.

Ian McMillan
May 1985

The illustrations are by Frank Thornton of Badge Group Design, Newcastle upon Tyne. Frank is a graphic designer and earlier in 1985 illustrated Rivelin Grapheme Press's collection of poetry "One + One".

Although the illustrations refer to a fraction of some of the poems, they are not necessarily adjacent to that poem or even that poet. A happy hour or two can be gainfully spent matching the several illustrations to the individual poems.

First published in 1985
by Rivelin Grapheme Press
199 Greyhound Road London W14 9SD

Printed in England by The Eastern Press Limited, Katesgrove Lane,
Reading, Berkshire.
Typeset by Wessex Typesetters, Frome, Somerset

British Library Cataloguing in Publication Data

Six: The Versewagon Poetry Manual
  1. English Poetry – 20th Century
  1. McMillan Ian
  821' .914'08   **PR1225**
  ISBN 0–947612–13–0 hard back
  ISBN 0–947612–14–9 paperback

Of this edition 26 copies in hardback have been lettered A–Z and signed by
the six authors.

 Rivelin Grapheme Press 1985